THE COLUMBIA GRANGER'S® GUIDE TO POETRY ANTHOLOGIES

Second Enlarged Edition

THE COLUMBIA GRANGER'S®
GUIDE TO POETRY
ANTHOLOGIES

Second Enlarged Edition

WILLIAM KATZ
LINDA STERNBERG KATZ
ESTHER CRAIN

COLUMBIA UNIVERSITY PRESS
NEW YORK

Columbia University Press
New York   Chichester, West Sussex
Copyright © 1991, 1994 Columbia University Press
All rights reserved

Library of Congress Cataloging-in-Publication Data

Katz, William A., 1924–
    The Columbia Granger's guide to poetry anthologies / William Katz,
Linda Sternberg Katz, Esther Crain—2nd enlarged edition.
        p.   cm.
    "Based on the seventh, eighth, ninth, and tenth editions of
The Columbia Granger's index to poetry"—Pref.
    Includes bibliographical references and index.
    ISBN 0–231–10104–X
    1. Poetry—Collections—Bibliography.   2. English poetry—Bibliography.
I. Katz, Linda Sternberg.   II. Crain, Esther.   III. Hazen, Edith P.
Columbia Granger's index to poetry.   IV. Title.
Z7156.A1K38   1994
[PN1111]   94-6482
016.80881—dc20   CIP

♾

Casebound editions of Columbia University Press books are printed
on permanent and durable acid-free paper

Book design by Jennifer Dossin

Printed in the United States of America
c 10 9 8 7 6 5 4 3 2 1

CONTENTS

PREFACE TO THE SECOND ENLARGED EDITION   xxxi

African Poetry   1

The Heinemann Book of African Poetry in English. Adewale Maja-
Pearce, ed.   1
The Negritude Poets. Ellen Conroy Kennedy, ed.   1
The Penguin Book of South African Verse. Jack Cope and
Uys Krige, eds.   2
The Penguin Book of Southern African Verse. Stephen Gray, ed.   2
Poems from Black Africa. Langston Hughes, ed.   3
When My Brothers Come Home. Frank Mkalawile Chipasula, ed.   3

African-American Poetry   4

African-American Poetry of the Nineteenth Century. Joan R. Sherman, ed.   4
American Negro Poetry. Arna Bontemps, ed.   4
Black American Literature: Poetry. Darwin T. Turner, ed.   5
Black Out Loud. Arnold Adoff, ed.   5
The Black Poets. Dudley Randall, ed.   6
Black Sister. Erlene Stetson, ed.   6
The Book of American Negro Poetry. James Weldon Johnson, ed.   6
The Books of American Negro Spirituals. James Weldon Johnson and
J. Rosamond Johnson, eds.   7
Caroling Dusk. Countee Cullen, ed.   7
Celebrations. Arnold Adoff, ed.   8
Collected Black Women's Poetry. Joan R. Sherman, ed.   8
The Forerunners. Woodie King, Jr., ed.   9
Golden Slippers. Arna Bontemps, comp.   9
I Am the Darker Brother. Arnold Adoff, ed.   9
Jump Bad. Gwendolyn Brooks, ed.   10
The New Black Poetry. Clarence Major, ed.   10
New Black Voices. Abraham Chapman, ed.   11
New Negro Poets U.S.A. Langston Hughes, ed.   11
The Poetry of Black America. Arnold Adoff, ed.   12

The Poetry of the Negro, 1746–1970. Langston Hughes and Arna
  Bontemps, eds.   12
Shadowed Dreams. Maureen Honey, ed.   12
3000 Years of Black Poetry. Alan Lomax and Raoul Abdul, eds.   13

American Poetry: Comprehensive Collections   14

America Forever New. Sara Brewton and John E. Brewton, comps.   14
America in Poetry. Charles Sullivan, ed.   14
America Is Not All Traffic Lights. Alice Fleming, ed.   15
American Poetry. Gay Wilson Allen, Walter B. Rideout, and James K.
  Robinson, eds.   15
Anthology of American Poetry. George Gesner, ed.   15
The Best Loved Poems of the American People. Hazel Felleman, ed.   16
Early American Poetry. Jane Donahue Eberwein, ed.   16
The Gift Outright. Helen Plotz, ed.   17
The Little Treasury of American Poetry. Oscar Williams, ed.   17
The Mentor Book of Major American Poets. Oscar Williams and Edwin
  Honig, eds.   18
The New Oxford Book of American Verse. Richard Ellmann, ed.   18
*The New Pocket Anthology of American Verse from Colonial Days to the
  Present.* Oscar Williams, ed.   18
The Oxford Book of American Verse. F. O. Matthiessen, ed.   19
Patriotic Poems America Loves. Jean Anne Vincent, comp.   19
Poems of American History. Burton Egbert Stevenson, ed.   20
The Poet in America, 1650 to the Present. Albert Gelpi, ed.   20
Six American Poets. Joel Connaroe, ed.   21
The Treasury of American Poetry. Nancy Sullivan, ed.   21

American Poetry: 17th, 18th, 19th Centuries   22

An American Anthology, 1787–1900. Edmund Clarence Stedman, ed.   22
American Poetry: the Nineteenth Century. John Hollander, ed.   22
American Verse of the Nineteenth Century. Richard Gray, ed.   23
Cowboy Poetry. Hal Cannon, ed.   23
101 Patriotic Poems.   24
Seventeenth-Century American Poetry. Harrison T. Meserole, ed.   25

American Poetry: 20th Century   26

The Actualist Anthology. Morty Sklar and Darrell Gray, eds.   26
The American Poetry Anthology. Daniel Halpern, ed.   26
American Poetry since 1970: Up Late. Andrei Codrescu, ed.   27
The Ardis Anthology of New American Poetry. David Rigsbee and Ellendea
  Proffer, eds.   27

The Jazz Poetry Anthology. Sascha Feinstein and
Yusef Komunyakaa, eds. 91
Modern Ballads and Story Poems. Charles Causley, ed. 91
One Hundred English Folksongs. Cecil J. Sharp, ed. 92
The Oxford Book of Ballads. James Kinsley, ed. 92
The Oxford Book of English Traditional Verse. Frederick Woods, ed. 93
The Penguin Book of Ballads. Geoffrey Grigson, ed. 93
Poems of the Old West. Levette J. Davidson, ed. 94
Popular Songs of Nineteenth Century America. Richard Jackson, ed. 94
The Richard Dyer-Bennet Folk Song Book. Richard Dyer-Bennet, ed. 94
The Ring of Words. Philip L. Miller, ed. 95
Shantymen and Shantyboys. William Main Doerflinger, ed. 95
Songs of Work and Protest. Edith Fowke and Joe Glazer, eds. 96
A Treasury of American Song. Olin Downes and Elie Siegmeister, eds. 96
The Viking Book of Folk Ballads of the English-Speaking World. Albert B.
Friedman, ed. 97
Yankee Doodles. Ted Malone, ed. 97

Canadian Poetry 98

Canadian Poetry in English. Bliss Carman, Lorne Pierce, and V. B.
Rhodenizer, eds. 98
Modern Canadian Verse. A. J. M. Smith, ed. 98
New American and Canadian Poetry. John Gill, ed. 99
The New Oxford Book of Canadian Verse in English. Margaret
Atwood, comp. 99
The Oxford Book of Canadian Verse in English and French. A. J. M.
Smith, ed. 100
The Penguin Book of Canadian Verse. Ralph Gustafson, ed. 100
The Wind Has Wings. Mary Alice Downie and
Barbara Robertson, eds. 100

Children's Poetry 102

Amazing Monsters. Robert Fisher, ed. 102
The Batsford Book of Light Verse for Children. Gavin Ewart, ed. 102
The Book of a Thousand Poems. J. Murray Macbain, ed. 103
A Book of Animal Poems. William Cole, ed. 103
Catch Your Breath. Lilian Moore and Lawrence Webster, eds. 103
A Child's Treasury of Verse. Eleanor Doan, ed. 104
Come Hither. Walter de la Mare, comp. 104
Ducks and Dragons. Gene Kemp, ed. 105
Dusk to Dawn. Helen Hill, Agnes Perkins, and Alethea Helbig, eds. 105
Every Child's Book of Verse. Sarah Chokla Gross, comp. 105
Everybody Ought to Know. Ogden Nash, ed. 106

The Faber Book of Children's Verse. Janet Adam Smith, comp.   106
A First Poetry Book. John Foster, comp.   107
Gladly Learn and Gladly Teach. Helen Plotz, ed.   107
The Home Book of Verse for Young Folks. Burton Egbert
  Stevenson, ed.   107
I Like You, If You Like Me. Myra Cohn Livingston, ed.   108
I Saw Esau. Iona Opie and Peter Opie, eds.   108
Imaginary Gardens. Charles Sullivan, ed.   109
In the Witch's Kitchen. John E. Brewton, Lorraine A. Blackburn, and
  George M. Blackburn III, comps.   109
Listen, Children, Listen. Myra Cohn Livingston, ed.   109
Messages. Naomi Lewis, comp.   110
The Moon Is Shining Bright as Day. Ogden Nash, ed.   110
Mother Goose Nursery Rhymes. Arthur Rackham, ed.   111
New Coasts & Strange Harbors. Helen Hill and Agnes Perkins, eds.   111
A New Treasury of Children's Poetry. Joanna Cole, comp.   112
A New Treasury of Poetry. Neil Philip, ed.   112
Of Quarks, Quasars, and Other Quirks. Sara Brewton, John E. Brewton,
  and John Brewton Blackburn, eds.   113
Oh, Such Foolishness! William Cole, ed.   113
Once upon a Rhyme. Sara Corrin and Stephen Corrin, eds.   113
The Oxford Book of Children's Verse. Iona Opie and Peter Opie, eds.   114
The Oxford Book of Children's Verse in America. Donald Hall, ed.   114
The Oxford Book of Story Poems. Michael Harrison and Christopher
  Stuart-Clark, eds.   115
The Oxford Nursery Rhyme Book. Iona Opie and Peter Opie, comps.   115
Piping Down the Valleys Wild. Nancy Larrick, ed.   116
Pocket Poems. Paul B. Janeczko, ed.   116
Poems for Children and Other People. George Hornby, ed.   116
Poems for Young Children. Caroline Royds, comp.   117
Poems to Read Aloud. Edward Hodnett, ed.   117
The Poet's Tales. William Cole, ed.   118
The Random House Book of Poetry for Children. Jack Prelutsky, ed.   118
Read-Aloud Rhymes for the Very Young. Jack Prelutsky, comp.   119
The Real Mother Goose. Blanche Fisher Wright, illust.   119
A Rocket in My Pocket. Carl Withers, comp.   120
Round about Eight. Geoffrey Palmer and Noel Lloyd, eds.   120
Saturday's Children. Helen Plotz, comp.   120
Shrieks at Midnight. Sara Brewton and John E. Brewton, eds.   121
Sing a Song of Popcorn. Beatrice Schenk de Regniers, Eva Moore, Mary
  Michaels White, and Jan Carr, eds.   121
Speak Roughly to Your Little Boy. Myra Cohn Livingston, ed.   122
Straight On Till Morning. Helen Hill, Agnes Perkins, and Alethea
  Helbig, comps.   122

Sung under the Silver Umbrella. Association for Childhood Education
    International editors, comps. 123
Talking like the Rain. X. J. Kennedy and Dorothy M. Kennedy, eds. 123
Talking to the Sun. Kenneth Koch and Kate Farrell, eds. 123
These Small Stones. Norma Farber and Myra Cohn Livingston,
    comps. 124
They've Discovered a Head in the Box for the Bread and Other Laughable
    Limericks. John E. Brewton and Lorraine A. Blackburn, eds. 124
This Delicious Day. Paul B. Janeczko, comp. 125
This Same Sky. Naomi Shihab Nye, ed. 125
Time for Poetry. May Hill Arbuthnot, ed. 126
Untune the Sky. Helen Plotz, comp. 126
Who Has Seen the Wind? Kathryn Sky-Peck, ed. 126
Why Am I Grown So Cold? Myra Cohn Livingston, ed. 127
The Year Around. Alice I. Hazeltine and Elva S. Smith, eds. 127
A Zooful of Animals. William Cole, ed. 128

Chinese Poetry 129

Among the Flowers. Lois Fusek, tr. 129
The Book of Songs. Arthur Waley, tr. 129
The Columbia Book of Chinese Poetry from Early Times to the Thirteenth
    Century. Burton Watson, ed. and tr. 130
The Columbia Book of Later Chinese Poetry. Jonathan Chaves,
    ed. and tr. 130
The Isle Full of Noises. Dominic Cheung, ed. and tr. 131
Literature of the Hundred Flowers. Vol. II: Poetry and Fiction. Hualing
    Nieh, ed. 131
One Hundred More Poems from the Chinese. Kenneth Rexroth,
    ed. and tr. 132
Poems of the Late T'ang. Arthur Charles Graham, ed. and tr. 132
A Splintered Mirror. Donald Finkel and Carolyn Kizer, eds. 133
Sunflower Splendor. Wu-chi Liu and Irving Yucheng Lo, eds. 133
Waiting for the Unicorn. Irving Yucheng Lo and
    William Schultz, eds. 134
Women Poets of China. Kenneth Rexroth and Ling Chung,
    eds. and trs. 134
Zen Poems of China & Japan. Lucien Stryk, Takashi Ikemoto, and
    Taigan Takayama, trs. 135

Death Poetry 136

Death in Literature. Robert F. Weir, ed. 136

Blood to Remember. Charles Fishman, ed. 28
The Bread Loaf Anthology of Contemporary American Poetry. Robert Pack,
  Sydney Lea, and Jay Parini, eds. 28
Brother Songs. Jim Perlman, ed. 29
California Bicentennial Poets Anthology. A. D. Winans, ed. 29
Contemporary American Poetry. Donald Hall, ed. 30
Contemporary American Poetry. A. Poulin, Jr., ed. 30
The Contemporary American Poets. Mark Strand, ed. 31
Contemporary Northwest Writing. Roy Carlson, ed. 31
Contemporary Poetry in America. Miller Williams, ed. 31
Contemporary Southern Poetry. Guy Owen and Mary C. Williams, eds. 32
A Controversy of Poets. Paris Leary and Robert Kelly, eds. 32
The Criterion Book of Modern American Verse. W. H. Auden, ed. 33
Divided Light: Father & Son Poems. Jason Shinder, ed. 33
Do Not Go Gentle. Michael Hogan, ed. 34
Don't Forget to Fly. Paul B. Janeczko, comp. 34
An Ear to the Ground. Marie Harris and Kathleen Aguero, eds. 35
Ecstatic Occasions, Expedient Forms. David Lehman, ed. 35
*Editor's Choice; Literature and Graphics from the Small U.S. Press, 1965–
  1977.* Morty Sklar and Jim Mulac, eds. 35
The Face of Poetry. LaVerne Harrell Clark and Mary MacArthur, eds. 36
15 Chicago Poets. Richard Friedman, Peter Kostakis, and Darlene
  Pearlstein, eds. 36
Fifty Contemporary Poets. Alberta T. Turner, ed. 37
Fifty Years of American Poetry. Introduction by Robert Penn Warren 37
Flowering after Frost. Michael McMahon, ed. 38
The Generation of 2000. William Heyen, ed. 38
A Geography of Poets. Edward Field, ed. 38
The Golden Year. Melville Cane, John Farrar, and
  Louise Nicholl, eds. 39
A Green Place. William Jay Smith, comp. 39
The Harvard Book of Contemporary American Poetry.
  Helen Vendler, ed. 40
Heartland II. Lucien Stryk, ed. 40
In the American Tree. Ron Silliman, ed. 40
"Language" Poetries. Douglas Messerli, ed. 41
The Longman Anthology of Contemporary American Poetry. Stuart Friebert
  and David Young, eds. 41
The Made Thing. Leon Stokesbury, ed. 42
Mark in Time. Nick Harvey and Robert E. Johnson, eds. 42
Mid-Century American Poets. John Ciardi, ed. 43
Modern American Poetry. Louis Untermeyer, ed. 43

Modern Poetry of Western America. Clinton F. Larson and William
  Stafford, eds.   44
The Morrow Anthology of Younger American Poets. Dave Smith and David
  Bottoms, eds.   44
Naked Poetry. Stephen Berg and Robert Mesey, eds.   45
The New American Poetry, 1945–1960. Donald M. Allen, ed.   45
New American Poets of the 80s. Jack Myers and Roger
  Weingarten, eds.   46
New American Poets of the '90s. Jack Myers and Roger
  Weingarten, eds.   46
A New Geography of Poets. Edward Field, Gerald Locklin, and Charles
  Stetler, eds.   47
The New Naked Poetry. Stephen Berg and Robert Mesey, eds.   47
New Poems by American Poets. Rolfe Humphries, ed.   48
New Poems by American Poets #2. Rolfe Humphries, ed.   48
New Poetry of the American West. Peter Wild and Frank Graziano, eds. 48
New Voices in American Poetry. David Allan Evans, ed.   49
New York: Poems. Howard Moss, ed.   49
The Next World. Joseph Bruchac, ed.   49
19 New American Poets of the Golden Gate. Philip Dow, ed.   50
The Pittsburgh Book of Contemporary American Poetry. Ed Ochester and
  Peter Oresick, eds.   50
The Poet Upstairs. Octave Stevenson, ed.   51
Poetry Hawaii. Frank Stewart and John Unterecker, eds.   51
The Poet's Choice. George E. Murphy, Jr., ed.   51
Poets West. Lawrence P. Spingarn, ed.   52
The Portable Beat Reader. Ann Charters, ed.   52
The Postmoderns. Donald Allen and George F. Butterick, eds.   53
Preferences. Richard Howard, ed.   53
Settling America. David Kherdian, ed.   54
70 on the 70's. Robert McGovern and Richard Snyder, eds.   54
Singular Voices. Stephen Berg, ed.   55
Strong Measures. Philip Dacey and David Jauss, eds.   55
Take Hold! Lee Bennett Hopkins, comp.   56
The Third Coast. Conrad Hilberry, Herbert Scott, and James Tipton,
  eds.   56
Traveling America with Today's Poets. David Kherdian, ed.   57
Twentieth-Century American Poetry. Conrad Aiken, ed.   57
Under 35. Nicholas Christopher, ed.   57
The Vintage Book of Contemporary American Poetry.
  J. D. McClatchy, ed.   58
Visions of America by the Poets of Our Time. David Kherdian, ed.   58
The Voice That Is Great within Us. Hayden Carruth, ed.   59
Washington and the Poet. Francis Coleman Rosenberger, ed.   59

American Poetry: 20th Century (Periodical)   60

The Antaeus Anthology. Daniel Halpern, ed.   60
Anthology of Magazine Verse and Yearbook of American Poetry, 1981 Edition.
   Alan F. Pater, ed.   60
The Before Columbus Foundation Poetry Anthology. J. J. Phillips, Ishmael
   Reed, Gundars Strads, and Shawn Wong, eds.   61
The Best American Poetry, 1988. John Ashbery, ed.   61
The Best American Poetry, 1989. Donald Hall, ed.   62
The Best American Poetry, 1990. Jorie Graham, ed.   62
The Best American Poetry, 1993. Louise Glück, ed.   63
From A to Z. David Ray, ed.   63
The Hopwood Anthology. Harry Thomas and Steven Lavine, eds.   63
Keener Sounds. Stanley W. Lindberg and Stephen Corey, eds.   64
Leaving the Bough. Roger Gaess, ed.   64
The New Yorker Book of Poems. The New Yorker editors, comps.   65
The Ploughshares Poetry Reader. Joyce Peseroff, ed.   65
The Poetry Anthology, 1912–1977. Daryl Hine and Joseph Parisi, eds.   66

Animal and Bird Poetry   67

Bear Crossings. Anne Newman and Julie Suk, eds.   67
Cat Will Rhyme with Hat. Jean Chapman, comp.   67
Fellow Mortals. Roy Fuller, comp.   68
Good Dog Poems. William Cole, comp.   68
Mice Are Rather Nice. Vardine Moore, comp.   69
101 Favorite Cat Poems. Sara L. Whittier, comp.   69
The Oxford Book of Animal Poems. Michael Harrison and Christopher
   Stuart-Clark, eds.   69
The Penguin Book of Bird Poetry. Peggy Munsterberg, ed.   70
The Poetry of Birds. Samuel Carr, ed.   70
The Poetry of Cats. Samuel Carr, ed.   71
The Poetry of Horses. William Cole, comp.   71
The Sophisticated Cat. Joyce Carol Oates and Daniel Halpern, comps.   71

Arabic Poetry   73

Arabic & Persian Poems. Omar S. Pound, ed. and tr.   73
Modern Arabic Poetry. Salma Khadra Jayyusi, ed.   73
Modern Poetry of the Arab World. Abdullah al-Udhari, ed. and tr.   74

Asian-American Poetry   75

Breaking Silence. Joseph Bruchac, ed.   75
The Open Boat. Garrett Hongo, ed.   75

Australasian Poetry   77

  An Anthology of Twentieth-Century New Zealand Poetry. Vincent
    O'Sullivan, comp.   77
  The Collins Book of Australian Poetry. Rodney Hall, comp.   77
  The Faber Book of Modern Australian Verse. Vincent Buckley, ed.   78
  The First Paperback Poets Anthology. Roger McDonald, ed.   78
  The Golden Apples of the Sun. Chris Wallace-Crabbe, ed.   79
  A Map of Australian Verse. James McAuley, ed.   79
  The New Oxford Book of Australian Verse. Les A. Murray, ed.   80
  The Oxford Book of Contemporary New Zealand Poetry. Fleur
    Adcock, comp.   80
  The Penguin Book of New Zealand Verse. Ian Wedde and Harvey
    McQueen, eds.   80
  Poetry in Australia. T. Inglis Moore and Douglas Stewart, comps.   81

Austrian Poetry   82

  Contemporary Austrian Poetry. Beth Bjorklund, ed. and tr.   82

Ballads and Songs   83

  American Folk Poetry. Duncan Emrich, ed.   83
  The American Songbag. Carl Sandburg, comp.   83
  As I Walked Out One Evening. Helen Plotz, ed.   84
  The Ballad Book. MacEdward Leach, ed.   84
  Best Loved Poems of the American West. John J. Gregg and Barbara T.
    Gregg, eds.   85
  Best Loved Songs and Hymns. James Morehead and Albert
    Morehead, eds.   85
  Best Loved Songs of the American People. Denes Agay, ed.   86
  The Blues Line. Eric Sackheim, ed.   86
  Breathes There the Man. Frank S. Meyer, ed.   87
  The Common Muse. Vivian de Sola Pinto and
    Allan Edwin Rodway, eds.   87
  Cowboy Songs and Other Frontier Ballads. John A. Lomax and Alan
    Lomax, eds.   88
  English and Scottish Ballads. Robert Graves, ed.   88
  English and Scottish Popular Ballads. Helen Sargent Child and George
    Lyman Kittredge, eds.   89
  The Faber Book of Ballads. Matthew Hodgart, ed.   89
  Favorite Songs of the Nineties. Robert A. Fremont, ed.   90
  Folksinger's Wordbook. Irwin Silber and Fred Silber, eds.   90
  The Illustrated Border Ballads. John Marsden, ed.   90